Mel Bay Presents

101 Three-Chord Children's Songs

for Guitar, Banjo, and Uke

by Larry McCabe

G000078395

1 2 3 4 5 6 7 8 9 0

Visit us on the Web at www.melbay.com — E-mail us at email@melbay.com

CONTENTS

CHORDS USED IN THIS BOOK

X Do not play this string   **1** First finger (index)   **3** Third finger (ring)

O Play this string open   **2** Second finger (middle)   **4** Fourth finger (little)

You can accompany every song in every song in this book using only three chords: G, C, and D7!

GUITAR CHORDS

Beginning guitar players can start with the chords shown at the right:

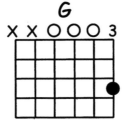 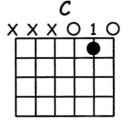 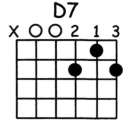

You can also play the "complete" C and G chords shown at the right. Notice that there are two possible fingerings for the six-string G.

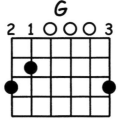 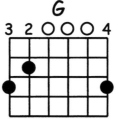 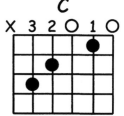

5-STRING BANJO CHORDS

The open fifth string (not shown) can be strummed with both G and C. It sounds better if the fifth string is omitted when strumming D7.

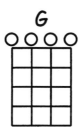 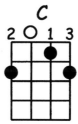 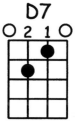

UKULELE CHORDS

Tune the uke G-C-E-A. Tip: The first finger (index) holds down (barres) three strings when playing D7.

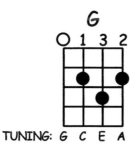 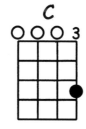 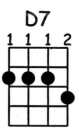

THE D CHORD

Pro tip: It is often possible to use a D chord (right) in place of D7. You can do this any time you feel that the sound of the music is improved by the substitution.

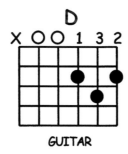 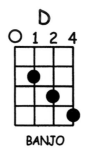 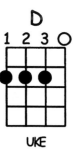

GUITAR   BANJO   UKE

3

EASY CHORD STRUMS

• You can strum chords with either a pick or your thumb.
• Play any chord(s) you like to practice these easy strums.

4/4 means "four beats to the measure." The easiest way to play in 4/4 is to strum four times in each measure. Use a down-pick motion ⊓ and count "one two three four," strumming a chord on each count:

Strum twice in each measure for songs in 2/4 time: Strum three times per measure for songs in 3/4 time:

The simple 2/4 strum above can also be used in *cut time* ¢ (cut time also has two beats per measure).

The plain *downbeat* strum can be livened up by adding *upbeat* strums. Pick the upbeat strums with an upward motion of the pick ∨ (or thumb, if you are strumming with your thumb). The following example, in 4/4 time, is counted "one and two and three and four and":

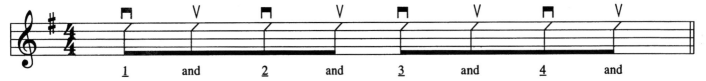

For variety, combine quarter-note strums with eighth-note strums. The next two examples show possibilities in 3/4 time:

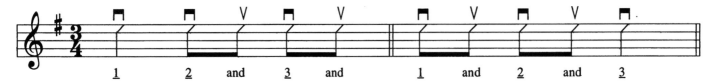

Here are two typical "combination strums" in 4/4 time:

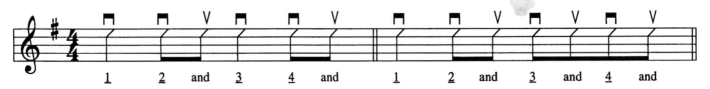

And two basic strums for 6/8 time:

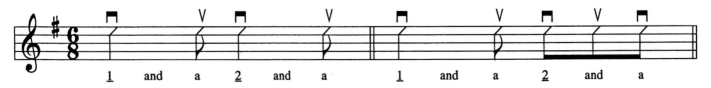

5-STRING BANJO ROLLS

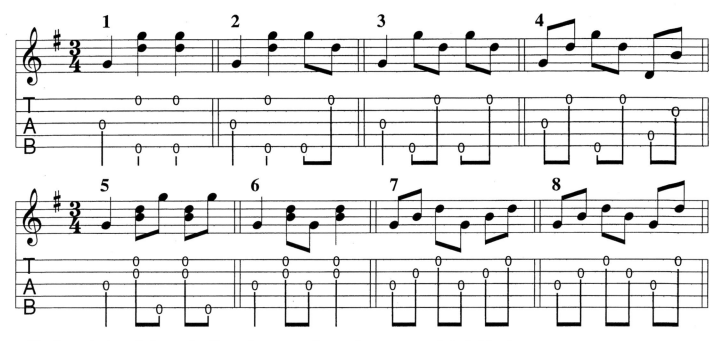

4/4 rolls can also be applied to *cut time*. For cut time, tap your foot two times per measure instead of four times.

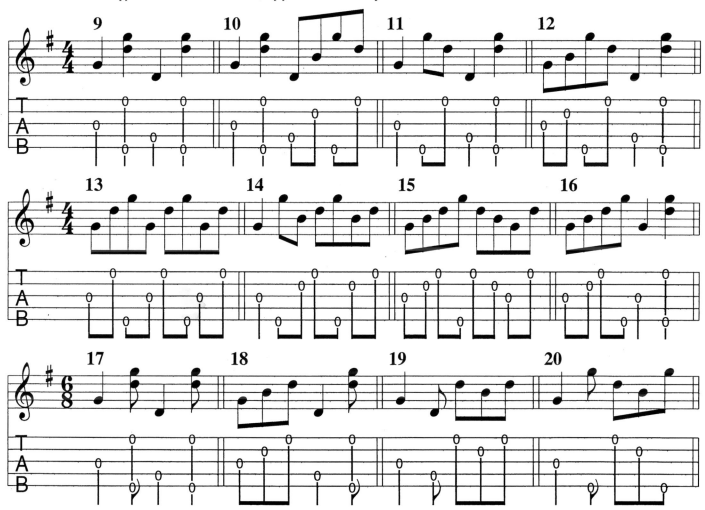

SINGING THE SONGS

THE STARTING NOTE

A "starting note" is given at the beginning of each song. <u>The starting note is the pitch of the first note of the song as it relates to the guitar</u>. For example, if the starting note is the "open fourth string," you can pluck that guitar string to hear the first note of the song.

A five-string banjo can also be used to find the starting note for songs that start on strings 2, 3, and 4. Our "starting note" concept cannot be applied to ukuleles.

CHANGING THE OCTAVE OR THE KEY

All the songs in this book are in the key of G major. Singers will sometimes find it helpful to sing a song one octave lower or higher than it is written. After deciding on the octave for the starting note, sing through several bars of the song to see if the melody "fits" your voice.

All singers will find that, for some songs, the key of G is not their best vocal key. If a song is difficult to sing in G, the guitarist can use a *capo* (a simple clamp, available at any music store) to *transpose* from G to a more suitable vocal key. The capo is placed at the appropriate fret (see below), and the picker can still strum the G, C, and D7 chords without having to learn new chord fingerings in new keys.

It is sometimes desirable to change keys for the purpose of accomodating an instrumentalist.

Ukulele players can use a capo, too (use a mandolin capo if you can't find a uke capo). Banjo players can use a capo, but the fifth string must also be capoed with a special *fifth-string capo*.

USING THE CAPO TO CHANGE KEYS

Each fret represents a half-step increase in pitch. Therefore, if the capo is placed at the first fret, and the chords are played in G, the actual key will be A-flat (A-flat is one-half step higher than G).

The following list shows the "actual" key when the capo is used while playing chords in the key of G:

First fret = Key of <u>A flat</u>

Second fret = Key of <u>A</u>

Third fret = Key of <u>B flat</u>

Fourth fret = Key of <u>B</u>

Fifth fret = Key of <u>C</u>

<u>In practice, the capo is seldom used beyond the fifth fret</u>. Nevertheless, here are some higher capo positions as they relate to the key of G:

Sixth fret = Key of <u>D flat</u>

Seventh fret = Key of <u>D</u>

Eighth fret = Key of <u>E flat</u>

Ninth fret = Key of <u>E</u>

Tenth fret = Key of <u>F</u>

Of course, another way to change keys is to transpose the melody and chords to the new key, and play the chords in the new key instead of using the capo. The subject of transposing without using a capo is beyond the scope of this book; see a music teacher if you are not sure how to do this.

The Alphabet Song

Starting note: Open third string.

The Animal Fair

Starting note: Fifth string, second fret.

I went to the an - i - mal fair,_____ The
birds and the beasts were there,_____ The
old ra - coon by the light of the moon Was
comb - ing his yel - low hair;_____ The
fun - ni - est was the monk,_____ Who
climbed up the el - e - phant's trunk;_____ The
el - e - phant sneezed and fell on his knees, and
what be - came of the monk?_____

Said a flea to a fly in a flue,
Said the flea, "Oh, what shall we do?"
Said the fly, "Let us flee," Said the flea, "Let us fly,"
So they flew thru a flaw in the flue.

The lion made a bow, and tried to kiss the cow,
The cow refused with several moos, which made the lion howl;
The parrots in the trees were watching chimpanzees,
The chimps were shy and covered their eyes and swung on the high trapeze.

A-Tiskit, A-Tasket

Starting note: Second string, third fret.

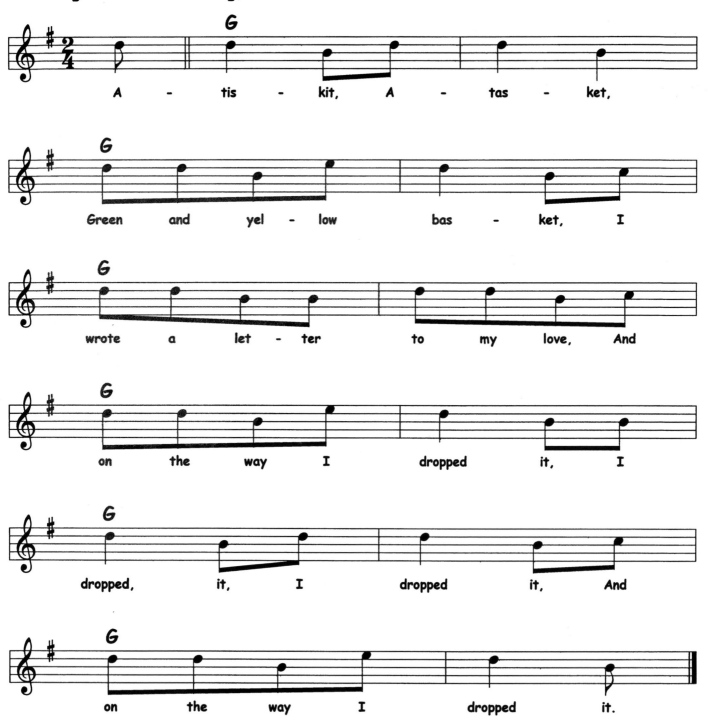

Children stand in a circle. When the words "I dropped it" are sung, a letter or handkerchief is dropped behind some child by another who runs around the circle of players as they sing. This child picks it up and drops it behind some other child; this keeps up until every child has had the letter or handkerchief.

Baa! Baa! Black Sheep

Starting note: Open third string.

The Big Rock Candy Mountain

Starting note: Open second string.

On a sum-mer day in the month of May, a___ bur-ley bum came hik-ing, Down a

shad-y lane thru the sug-ar cane he was look-ing for his lik-ing; As he

roamed a-long he sang a song of the land of milk and hon-ey, Where a

bum can stay for___ man-y a day, and he won't need an-y mon-ey. Oh, the

buz-zin' of the bees in the can-dy bar trees near the so-da wat-er foun-tain; At the

lem-on-ade springs where the blue-bird sings, In the Big Rock Can-dy Moun-tain.

On a run came a farmer and his son, to the hayfields they were bounding,
Said the bum to the son "Why don't you come to that Big Rock Candy Mountain?"
So the mail train stops and there ain't no cops and the folks are tender* countin',
And they soon arrived at the lemonade tide in that Big Rock Candy Mountain.
Chorus

* Money

B-I-N-G-O

Starting note: Open fourth string.

There was a farm-er had a dog and Bin-go was his name-o,

B - I - N - G - O,   B - I - N - G - O,

B - I - N - G - O, And Bin-go was his name, oh!

Each time the song is repeated, a hand clap replaces a letter in the word B-I-N-G-O:

2. (CLAP)-I-N-G-O,
   (CLAP)-I-N-G-O,
   (CLAP)-I-N-G-O,
   And Bingo was his name, oh!

3. (CLAP)-(CLAP)-N-G-O,
   (CLAP)-(CLAP)-N-G-O,
   (CLAP)-(CLAP)-N-G-O,
   And Bingo was his name, oh!

4. (CLAP)-(CLAP)-(CLAP)-G-O,
   (CLAP)-(CLAP)-(CLAP)-G-O,
   (CLAP)-(CLAP)-(CLAP)-G-O,
   And Bingo was his name, oh!

5. (CLAP)-(CLAP)-(CLAP)-(CLAP)-(CLAP),
   (CLAP)-(CLAP)-(CLAP)-(CLAP)-(CLAP),
   (CLAP)-(CLAP)-(CLAP)-(CLAP)-(CLAP),
   And Bingo was his name, oh!

Black-Eyed Susie

Starting note: Second string, third fret.

All I want to make me happy,
Two little boys to call me pappy.
Chorus

Gonna go home with a sack full of money,
Someone there to call me honey.
Chorus

I love my wife, I love my lady,
Love my biscuits sopped in gravy.
Chorus

Black-Eyed Susie went to town,
Dressed up fine in a gingham gown.
Chorus

The Bold Fisherman

Starting note: Open fourth string.

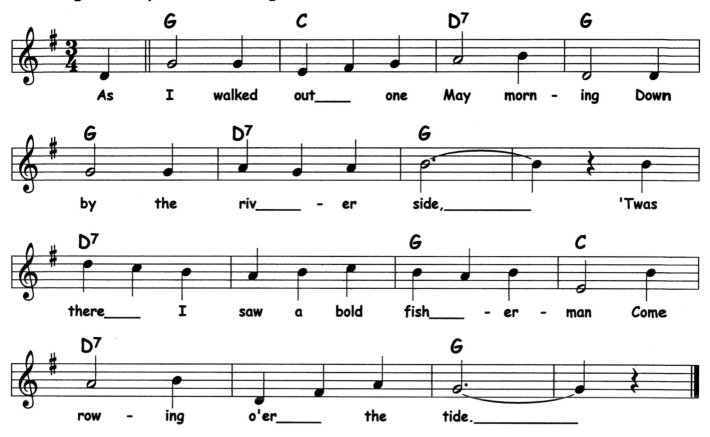

As I walked out____ one May morn - ing Down

by the riv____ - er side,_____ 'Twas

there____ I saw a bold fish____ - er - man Come

row - ing o'er____ the tide._____

"Bold fisherman, bold fisherman,
Why are you fishing here?"
"I've come for you, fair lady friend,
All down the river clear."

He took her by her lily-white hand,
Saying, "Follow, follow me";
"I'll take you to my father's house,
If you will marry me."

"Oh yes, oh yes, I'll marry you,"
The fair young maiden did say;
"For I have loved you for so long,
And with you forever I'll stay."

Brother John
(Frère Jacques)

Starting note: Open third string.

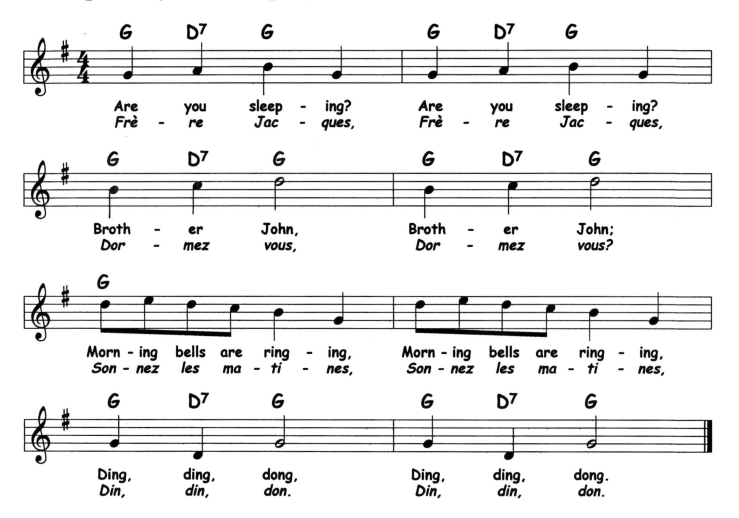

Are you sleep - ing? Are you sleep - ing?
Frè - re Jac - ques, Frè - re Jac - ques,

Broth - er John, Broth - er John;
Dor - mez vous, Dor - mez vous?

Morn - ing bells are ring - ing, Morn - ing bells are ring - ing,
Son - nez les ma - ti - nes, Son - nez les ma - ti - nes,

Ding, ding, dong, Ding, ding, dong.
Din, din, don. Din, din, don.

Calendar Song

Starting note: Fifth string, second fret.

Six - ty sec - onds make a min - ute, Some-thing sure you__ can learn in it;

Six - ty min - utes make an hour, Work with all your__ might and pow'r.

Twen - ty four hours make a day,___ Time e - nough for work and play;___

Sev - en days a week will make, You will learn if___ pains you take.

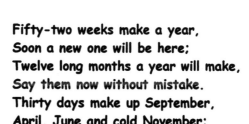

Fifty-two weeks make a year,
Soon a new one will be here;
Twelve long months a year will make,
Say them now without mistake.
Thirty days make up September,
April, June and cold November;
All the rest have thirty-one,
February stands alone.

Twenty-eight is all his share,
With twenty-nine in each Leap Year;
That you may the Leap-Year know,
Divide by four and that will show.
In each year are seasons four,
You will learn them, I am sure!
Spring and summer, then the fall,
Winter last, but best of all.

Chime Again, Beautiful Bells

Starting note: Open second string.

Henry Bishop

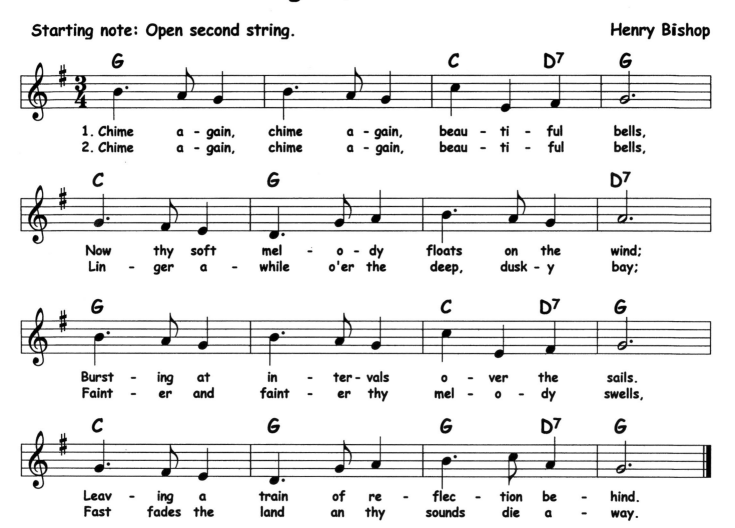

1. Chime a - gain, chime a - gain, beau - ti - ful bells,
2. Chime a - gain, chime a - gain, beau - ti - ful bells,

Now thy soft mel - o - dy floats on the wind;
Lin - ger a - while o'er the deep, dusk - y bay;

Burst - ing at in - ter - vals o - ver the sails.
Faint - er and faint - er thy mel - o - dy swells,

Leav - ing a train of re - flec - tion be - hind.
Fast fades the land an thy sounds die a - way.

Cindy

Starting note: Second string, third fret.

You ought to see my Cin - dy, She comes from way down South, And

she's so sweet, the hon - ey bees just swarm a - round her mouth; Get 'long

home, Cin - dy Cin - dy, Get 'long home, Cin - dy Cin - dy, Get 'long

home, Cin - dy, Cin - dy, I'll mar - ry you some day.

I wish I was an apple, hangin' on a tree,
And every time my Cindy's pass
She'd take a bite of me.
Chorus

I wish I was a needle, as fine as I could sew,
I'd sew myself to the girls' coattails
And down the road I'd go.
Chorus

When Cindy got religion
I'll tell you what she done;
She walked up to the preacher
And chawed her chewin' gum.
Chorus

Colinda

Starting note: Open fourth string.

Cajun Tune

Al - lons dans - er, Co-lin - da,____ Al - lons dans - er, Co-lin - da,____ Pen - dant ta

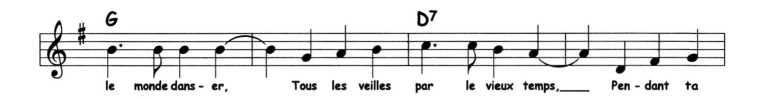

mère est past là,_____ Pour faire fach - er les vieilles femmes;__ C'est pas tout

le monde dans - er, Tous les veilles par le vieux temps,____ Pen - dant ta

mère est pas là,_____ Al - lons dans - er, Co - lin - da._____

Comin' Thru the Rye

Starting note: Open fourth string.

1. If a bod-y meet a bod-y, com-in' thru the rye,
2. If a bod-y meet a bod-y, com-in' thru the town,

If a bod-y kiss a bod-y, need a bod-y cry?
If a bod-y greet a bod-y, need a bod-y frown?

Ev-'ry las-sie has her lad-die, none, they say, have I, Yet

all the lads they smile at me when com-in' thru the rye.

The Cowboy's Dream

Starting note: Open fourth string.

The road to that bright happy region,
Is a dim, narrow trail so they say;
But the broad one that leads to perdition
Is posted and blazed all the way.
Chorus

They say there will be a great roundup,
And cowboys like dogies will stand;
To be cut by the riders of judgement,
Who are posted and know every brand.
Chorus

I wonder if ever a cowboy,
Stood ready for that judgement day;
And could say to the boss of the riders,
"I'm ready, come drive me away."
Chorus

The Cuckoo

Starting note: Second string, third fret.

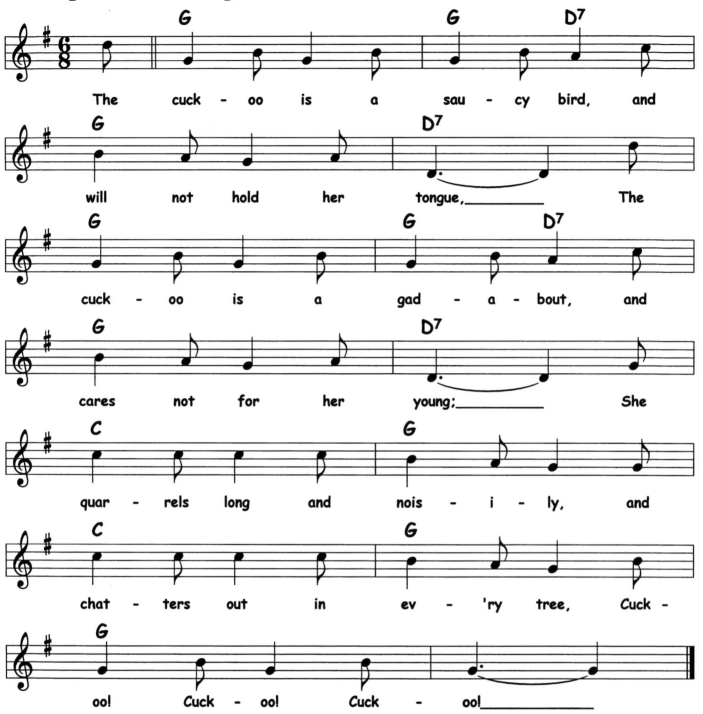

The cuck - oo is a sau - cy bird, and will not hold her tongue,_____ The cuck - oo is a gad - a - bout, and cares not for her young;_____ She quar - rels long and nois - i - ly, and chat - ters out in ev - 'ry tree, Cuck - oo! Cuck - oo! Cuck - oo!_____

The robin and the oriole oft scold her to her face,
They tell her faults to all the wood, and publish her disgrace;
Yet not a single whit cares she, but chirrups at them saucily,
Cuckoo! Cuckoo! Cuckoo!

The Fairy Ship

Starting note: Open fourth string.

The Farmer

Starting note: Open third string.

3. Shall I show you how the farmer . . .
   Reaps his barley and wheat.

4. Look 'tis thus, thus that the farmer . . .
   Reaps his barley and wheat.

5. Shall I show you how the farmer . . .
   Threshes barley and wheat.

6. Look, 'tis thus, thus that the farmer . . .
   Threshes barley and wheat.

The Farmer in the Dell

Starting note: Open fourth string.

The farm - er in the dell, The

farm - er in the dell;

Heigh, oh the der - ry oh, The

farm - er in the dell.

2. The farmer takes a wife . . .

3. The wife takes the child . . .

4. The child takes the nurse . . .

5. The nurse takes the dog . . .

6. The dog takes the cat . . .

7. The cat takes the rat . . .

8. The rat takes the cheese . . .

9. The cheese stands alone . . .

A child, representing the farmer, stands in the center of a circle of children, and chooses another child, "the wife," at the end of the second verse; this one choose another, "the child," and so on until "the cheese" is selected, after which the game begins over again.

The Fox

Starting note: Second string, third fret.

He ran 'til he came to a great big pen
Where the ducks and the geese were put there-in;
A couple of you will grease my chin
Before I leave this town-o.
Town-o . . .

He grabbed the gray goose by the neck,
Throwed the little ones o'er his back;
He didn't mind their quack, quack, quack,
With their legs all dangling down-o.
Down-o . . .

Well old mother flipper-flopper jumped out of bed,
Out of the window she cocked her head;
Crying, "John, John, the gray goose is gone,
And the fox is on the town-o."
Town-o . . .

Well, John he ran to the top of the hill,
Blowed his horn both loud and shrill;
The fox, he said, "I better flee with my kill,
Or they'll soon be on my trail-o."
Trail-o . . .

He ran 'til he came to his cozy den,
There were the little ones, eight, nine, ten;
They said, "Daddy, better go back again,
For it must be a mighty fine town-o."
Town-o . . .

So the fox and his wife without any strife,
Cut up the goose with a fork and knife;
They never had such a supper in their life,
And the little ones chewed on the bones-o.
Bones-o . . .

Free Little Bird

Starting note: Open fourth string.

I'm a free lit - tle bird as I can be, I can be, I'm a

free lit - tle bird as I can be; Gon - na

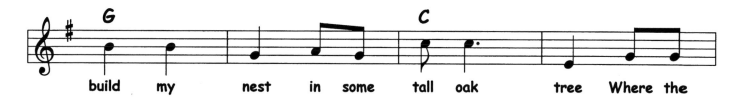

build my nest in some tall oak tree Where the

bad boys they can - not both - er me.

The first verse (above) is often treated as a chorus.

Carry me home, little birdie, carry me home, carry me home,
Carry me home, little birdie, carry me home;
Carry me home to my wife, she's the joy of my life,
Carry me home, little birdie, carry me home.
(*Chorus*)

I'll never build my nest on the ground, on the ground,
Oh, I'll never build my nest on the ground;
But I'll build my nest in a tall willow tree,
Where the bad boys cannot tear it down.
(*Chorus*)

Froggie Went a-Courtin'

Starting note: Open third string.

Frog-gie went a-court-in', he did ride, uh - huh,_____

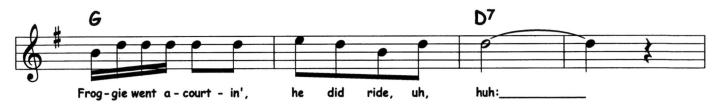

Frog-gie went a-court-in', he did ride, uh, huh:_____

Frog-gie went a-court-in', he did ride, Sword and a pis-tol by his side, Uh -

huh,_____ Uh, - huh._____

He rode right up to Miss Mousie's den, uh-huh,
Rode right up to Miss Mousie's den, uh-huh;
Rode right up to Miss Mousie's den,
Said, "Please, Miss Mousie, won't you let me in,"
Uh-huh, Uh-huh.

He said, "Miss Mousie, will you marry me?" Uh-huh,
Said, "Miss Mousie, will you marry me?" Uh-huh;
Said, "Miss Mousie, will you marry me,
Way down yonder in a hollow tree?"
Uh-huh, Uh-huh.

Where will the wedding supper be, uh-huh,
Where will the wedding supper be, uh-huh?
Where will the wedding supper be?
Way down yonder in the hollow tree,
Uh-huh, Uh-huh.

What will the wedding supper be, uh-huh?
What will the wedding supper be, uh-huh?
What will the wedding supper be?
Smoked hog jowls and black-eyed peas,
Uh-huh, Uh-huh.

First to come in was a bumblebee, uh-huh,
First to come in was a bumblebee, uh-huh;
First to come in was a bumblebee,
With a big bass fiddle restin' on his knee,
Uh-huh, Uh-huh.

Next to come in was a little gray mouse, uh-huh,
Next to come in was a little gray mouse, uh-huh;
Next to come in was a little gray mouse,
And he said, "Mr. Froggie, can I rent your house?"
Uh-huh, Uh-huh.

Froggie went a travelin' across the lake, uh-huh,
Froggie went a travelin' across the lake, uh-huh;
Froggie went a travelin' across the lake,
And he got swallowed up by a cottonmouth snake,
Uh-huh, Uh-huh.

German Cradle Song

Starting note: Open second string.

The Glendy Burk

Starting note: Open fourth string.

Stephen Foster

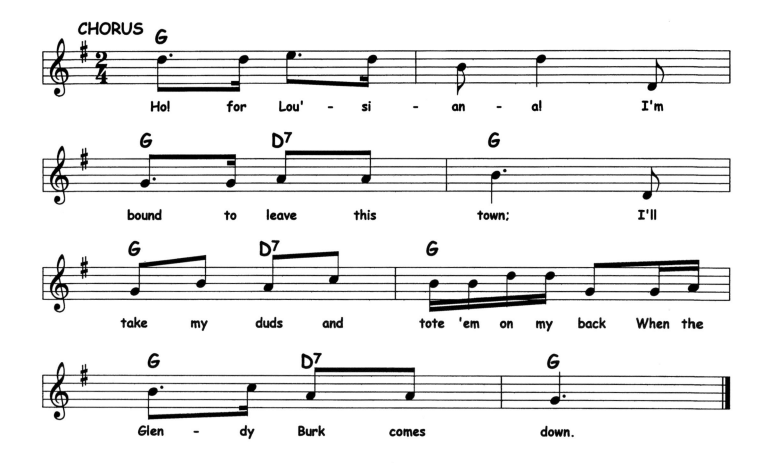

CHORUS

Ho! for Lou' - si - an - a! I'm bound to leave this town; I'll take my duds and tote 'em on my back When the Glen - dy Burk comes down.

The Glendy Burk has a funny crew
And they sing the boatman's song;
They burn the pitch and the pine knot too,
For to shove the boat along.
The smoke goes up and the engine roars,
And the wheel goes 'round and 'round;
So fare you well, for I'll take a little ride
When the Glendy Burk comes down.
Chorus

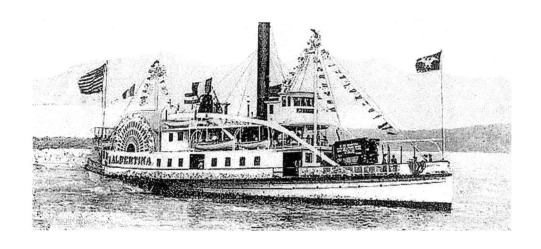

Goober Peas

Starting note: Open fourth string.

Civil War Song

2. When a horseman passes, the soldiers have a rule,
   To cry out at their loudest, "Mister, here's your mule!"
   But another pleasure enchantinger than these,
   Is wearing out your grinders, eating goober peas!
   Chorus

3. Just before the battle the Gen'ral hears a row,
   He says, "The Yanks are coming, I hear their rifles now;"
   He turns around in wonder, and whattaya think he sees?
   The Georgia militia, eating goober peas!
   Chorus

4. I think my song has lasted almost long enough,
   The subject's interesting, but rhymes are mighty rough;
   I wish this war was over, when free from rags and fleas,
   We'll kiss our wives and sweethearts, and gobble goober peas!
   Chorus

Goodnight, Ladies

Starting note: Open second string.

Good - night, la - dies, Good - night, la - dies;

Good - night, la - dies, We're going to leave you now.

Mer - ri - ly we roll a - long, Roll a - long, roll a - long;

Mer - ri - ly we roll a - long, O'er the deep blue sea.

Farewell ladies,
Farewell ladies;
Farewell ladies,
We're going to leave you now.
Chorus

Sweet dreams, ladies
Sweet dreams, ladies;
Sweet dreams, ladies,
We're going to leave you now.
Chorus

Green Corn

Starting note: Open second string.

All I need to make me happy,
Two little kids to call me pappy. (2x)

One named Bill, the other named Davy,
They like their biscuits sopped in gravy. (2x)

The Green Grass Grew All Around

Starting note: Open fourth string.

There was a tree, Oh, there was a tree, And the

tree was in the ground, In a hole in the ground; And the

green grass grew all a - round, all a - round, And the

green grass grew all a - round.

And on this tree there was a limb,
The prettiest limb that you ever did see,
And the tree was in the ground;
And the green grass grew all around, all around,
And the green grass grew all around.

And on this limb there was a branch,
The prettiest branch that you ever did see,
And the branch was in the tree;
And the green grass grew all around, all around,
And the green grass grew all around.

And on this branch there was a twig,
The prettiest twig that you ever did see,
And the twig was on the branch;
And the green grass grew all around, all around,
And the green grass grew all around.

And on this twig there was a leaf,
The prettiest leaf that you ever did see,
And the leaf was on the twig;
And the green grass grew all around, all around,
And the green grass grew all around.

And on this leaf there was a bird,
The prettiest bird that you ever did see,
And the bird was on the leaf;
And the green grass grew all around, all around,
And the green grass grew all around.

Home, Home, Can I Forget Thee?

Starting note: Open second string.

1. Home, home, can I for - get thee?
2. Home, home, why did I leave thee?

Dear, dear, dear - ly lov'd home;
Dear, dear, friends, do not mourn;

No, no, still I re - gret thee,
Home, home, once more re - ceive me,

Tho' I may far from thee roam._____
Quick - ly to thee I'll re - turn._____

Home, home, home, home,

dear - est and hap - pi - est home._____

How Old Are You?

Starting note: Open third string.

How old are you, my pret-ty lit-tle miss? How

old are you, my hon - ey? She

an - swered me with a sil - ly lit - tle smile, "I'll

be six - teen next Sun - day."

2. Where are you going, my pretty little miss?
Where are you going, my honey?
She answered my with a silly little smile,
"I'm looking for my mommie."

3. Will you marry me, my pretty little miss?
Will you marry me, my honey?
She answered with a silly little smile,
"I'll run and ask my mommie."

4. Where do you live, my pretty little miss?
Where do you live, my honey?
She answered with a silly little smile,
"I live on the hill with mommie."

5. Hey, come along, my pretty little miss,
Hey, come along, my honey;
She answered me with a silly little smile,
"I won't be home till Sunday."

Humpty Dumpty

Starting note: Open third string.

Hunter's Song

Starting note: Open third string.

I'm Going to Leave Old Texas

Starting note: Open fourth string.

I'm going to leave_____ old___ Tex - as now;_____ They've no more use_____ for the long - horned cow.

They've plowed and fenced the cattle range;
And people there are all so strange.

Saddle up my horse, take a look around;
I'm leaving here for another town.

I'll say goodbye to San Antone;
Maybe take the trail to Old Mexico.

It's Raining, It's Pouring

Starting note: Fifth string, second fret.

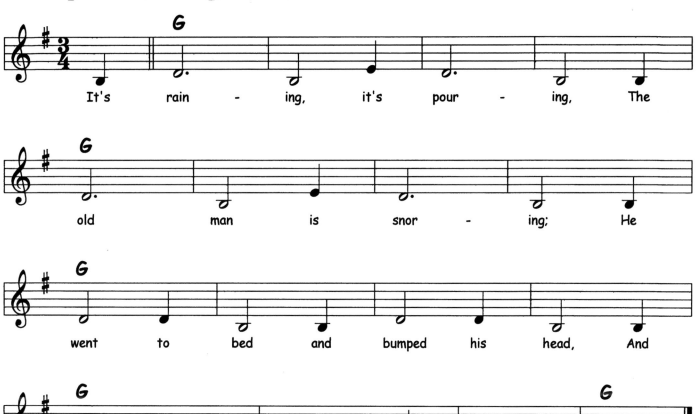

It's rain - ing, it's pour - ing, The

old man is snor - ing; He

went to bed and bumped his head, And

could not get up in the morn - ing.

The Itsy-Bitsy Spider

Starting note: Open fourth string.

The it - sy bit - sy spi - der went up the wa - ter spout,

Down came the rain_____ and washed the spi - der out;

Out came the sun and dried up all the rain, And the

it - sy bit - sy spi - der went up the spout a - gain.____

Finger Play While Singing

First line: "Walk" the fingers of one hand up the other hand or arm.

Second line: Lower the hands to make rain; wash spider from spout by placing hands together in front, then extend each hand/arm to the side.

Third line: Form the sun by holding arms in a circle over head.

Fourth line: Walk fingers of one hand up the other arm.

Jenny Jenkins

Starting note: Open second string.

Will you wear white, oh my dear, my dear, Will you wear white, Jen - ny Jen - kins? I won't wear white, for the col - or is too bright, I'll buy me a tal - ly wal - ly aye, sir.

Will you wear blue, oh my dear, my dear,
Will you wear blue, Jenny Jenkins?
I won't wear blue, for the color is too true,
I'll buy me a tally wally aye, sir.

Will you wear red, oh my dear, my dear,
Will you wear red, Jenny Jenkins?
I won't wear red, it's the color that I dread,
I'll buy me a tally wally aye, sir.

Will you wear green, oh my dear, my dear,
Will you wear green, Jenny Jenkins?
I won't wear green, for it's a shame to be seen,
I'll buy me a tally wally aye, sir.

Will you wear black, oh my dear, my dear,
Will you wear black, Jenny Jenkins?
I won't wear black, for it causes me bad luck,
I'll buy me a tally wally aye, sir.

Jenny Jones

Starting note: Open fourth string.

VERSE

We've come to see Miss Jen - ny Jones, Miss Jen - ny Jones, Miss Jen - ny Jones; We've
Miss Jen - ny is a - wash____ - ing, A - wash____ - ing, a - wash____ - ing; Miss

come to see Miss Jen - ny Jones, And how is she____ to - day?____
Jen - ny is a - wash____ - ing, You can't see her____ to - day.____

CHORUS

We're so glad to hear____ it, To hear____ it, to hear____ it;
(sorry)

We're so glad to hear____ it, And how is she____ to - day?____
(sorry)

2. We've come to see . . .
   Miss Jenny is a-starching . . .

3. We've come to see . . .
   Miss Jenny is a-ironing . . .

4. We've come to see . . .
   Miss Jenny is a-sweeping . . .

5. We've come to see . . .
   Miss Jenny has gone visiting . . .

6. We've come to see . . .
   Miss Jenny's at her uncle's farm . . .

7. We've come to see . . .
   Miss Jenny's grown and gone away . . .

One child represents Miss Jenny Jones and another child her mother. The players dance in a circle around them singing "We've come to see Miss Jenny Jones." The two children in the center answer "Miss Jenny Jones is a-washing," etc.

When the mother says "Miss Jenny's grown and gone away," the children run away in all directions crying. The first child that "Jenny" catches takes her place in the circle, and the game begins again.

John Jacob Jingleheimer Schmidt

Starting note: Open second string.

John   Ja - cob   Jin - gle - hei - mer Schmidt,

His   name   is   my   name   too;_____   When

ev - er   we   go   out,   the   peo - ple   al - ways shout,

"John   Ja - cob Jin - gle - hei - mer   Schmidt." Da - da - da - da - da - da - da.

Sing the song over and over according to your needs/endurance. The song ends on the word "Schmidt," on the first beat of the final measure.

Johnny Get Your Haircut

Starting note: Open third string.

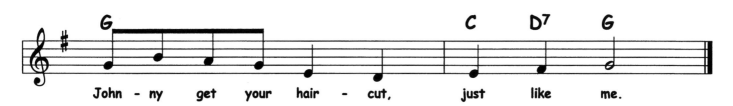

Johnny get your gun and your sword and your pistol,
Johnny get your gun, and come with me;
Johnny get your gun and your sword and your pistol,
Johnny get your gun, and come with me.

Hey, Betty Martin, tiptoe, tiptoe,
Hey, Betty Martin, tiptoe fine;
Hey, Betty Martin, tiptoe, tiptoe,
Hey, Betty Martin, tiptoe fine.

Johnny get your haircut, haircut, haircut,
Johnny get your haircut, just like me;
Johnny get your haircut, haircut, haircut,
Johnny get your haircut, just like me.

Juanita

Starting note: Second string, third fret.

Spanish Air
Words by Carolyn Norton

Soft   o'er the   foun - tain,   lin-g'ring falls   the   south-ern moon;
When   in thy   dream - ing,   Moons like these   shall   shine a - gain,

Far   o'er the   moun - tain,   breaks the day   too   soon.
And   day - light   beam - ing,   Prove thy dreams are   vain.

In   thy dark   eyes   splen - dor   Where the warm   light   loves to   dwell,
Wilt thou not,   re - lent - ing,   For thine ab - sent   lov - er   sigh,

Wea - ry   looks,   yet   ten - der   speak their fond   fare - well.
In thy heart   con - sent - ing   To   a   pray'r gone   by?

Ni - ta!   Jua_____ - ni - ta!   Ask thy soul   if   we should part!
Ni - ta!   Jua_____ - ni - ta!   Let me lin - ger   by thy side!

Ni - ta!   Jua_____ - ni - ta!   Lean   thou   on   my   heart.
Ni - ta!   Jua_____ - ni - ta!   Be   my own   fair   bride!

The King of France

Starting note: Open fourth string.

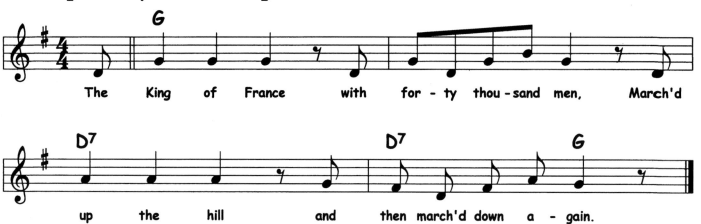

The King of France with for-ty thou-sand men, March'd

up the hill and then march'd down a-gain.

Two rows of children are formed, each with a leader and each facing the other. Each leader advances several steps, singing and matching their gestures to the words of the song. Then the two rows march toward each other, singing and imitating their leaders.

Lavender's Blue

Starting note: Open third string.

Lazy Mary

Starting note: Open third string.

No, no, Mother, I won't get up,
I won't get up, I won't get up;
No, no, Mother, I won't get up,
I won't get up today.

All the children sing the first verse, while dancing around the child
chosen to be "Lazy Mary." Then they all sing the second verse together.

Lightly Row

Starting note: Second string, third fret.

1. Light - ly row! light - ly row! O'er the glas - sy waves we go;
2. Far a - way! far a - way! Ech - o in the rock at play:

Smooth - ly glide! smooth - ly glide! on the si - lent tide.
Call - eth not, call - eth not, to this lone - ly spot.

Let the winds and wa - ters be min - gled with our child - ish glee,
On - ly with the sea - bird's note shall our hap - py mu - sic float,

Sing and float! sing and float! in our lit - tle boat.
Light - ly row! light - ly row! in our lit - tle boat.

Listen to the Mockingbird

Starting note: Open fourth string.

Septimus Winner

CHORUS

mock - ing - bird, Lis-ten to the mock-ing - bird, The mock - ing - bird still sing - ing o'er her grave; Lis-ten to the mock - ing - bird, Lis-ten to the mock - ing - bird, Still sing - ing where the weep - ing wil - lows wave.

Ah! well I yet remember,
Remember, remember,
Ah! well I yet remember,
When we gather'd in the cotton side by side;
'Twas in the mild September,
September, September,
'Twas in the mild September,
And the mockingbird was singing far and wide.
Chorus

When the charms of spring awaken,
Awaken, awaken,
When the charms of spring awaken,
And the mockingbird is singing in the bough;
I feel like one forsaken,
Forsaken, forsaken,
I feel like one forsaken,
Since my Hally is no longer with me now.
Chorus

The Little Lamb

Starting note: Open second string.

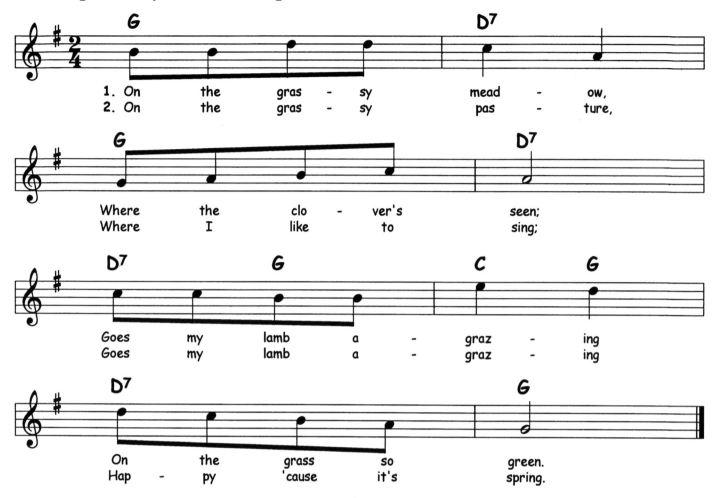

The Little Old Sod Shanty

Starting note: Second string, third fret.

London Bridge

Starting note: Second string, third fret.

Lon - don bridge is fall - ing down,

Fall - ing down, fall - ing down;

Lon - don bridge is fall - ing down,

My fair la - dy.

Build it up with iron bars,
Iron bars, iron bars;
Build it up with iron bars,
My fair lady.

Iron bars will bend and break,
Bend and break, bend and break;
Iron bars will bend and break,
My fair lady.

Build it up with silver and gold,
Silver and gold, silver and gold;
Build it up with silver and gold,
My fair lady.

The children pass under a bridge formed by two other children raising their arms to form an arch. These two children have previously secretly decided which one represents "gold" and which one "silver."

At the words "My fair lady," the bridge falls; that is, the children imitating it, drop their hands, and the child who is caught is asked which s/he prefers, "gold or silver."

This child then takes his place behind the one who represents his choice and the game continues until all have chosen. Finally, a tug-of-war between the "gold and silver" teams ends the game.

Looby Loo

Starting note: Open third string.

This English game can be played with many variations. For example, in place of the instruction "Put your right hand out," the players can substitute the right foot, the left foot, the head, etc.

While singing the song, the children join hands in a circle, swaying from side to side during the chorus, and performing the indicated actions during the verses.

Mama Don't Allow

Starting note: Open third string.

Ma - ma don't al - low no   mu - sic played in   here   (played in   here),

Ma - ma don't al - low no   mu - sic played in   here   (played in   here);

We don't care what   she don't al - low, gon - na play our mu - sic   an - y - how,

Ma - ma don't al - low no   mu - sic played in   here._____

Mama don't allow no guitar pickers in here . . .

Mama don't allow no piano pounders in here . . .

Mama don't allow no bass fiddlers in here . . .

Etc.

When performing this song, it is customary for the appropriate instrument to play an instrumental solo after each verse. If no instruments are available, the children may imitate the solos by performing with imaginary instruments.

Mary Wore Her Red Dress

Starting note: Open fourth string.

Mary wore a red hat, red hat, red hat;
Mary wore a red hat all day long.

Mary wore her red shoes, red shoes, red shoes;
Mary wore her red shoes all day long.

Mary wore her red gloves . . .

Mary made a red cake . . .

Where'd you get your shoes from? . . .

Got 'em from the dry goods . . .

Where'd you get your butter from? . . .

Got it from the grocery . . .

Mary wore a red skirt . . .

The Muffin Man

Starting note: Open fourth string.

Oh, do you know the muf - fin man, The
muf - fin man, the muf - fin man?
Do you know the muf - fin man Who
lives on Dru - ry Lane?

Oh, yes, we know the muffin man,
The muffin man, the muffin man;
Yes, we know the muffin man
Who lives on Drury Lane.

The Mulberry Bush

Starting note: Open third string.

Here we go round the mul - ber - ry bush, the

mul - ber - ry bush, the mul - ber - ry bush;

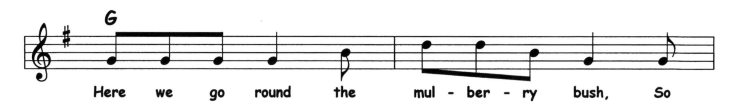

Here we go round the mul - ber - ry bush, So

ear - ly in____ the morn - ing.

2. This is the way we wash our clothes,
   Wash our clothes, wash our clothes;
   This is the way we wash our clothes,
   So early Monday morning.

3. This is the way we iron our clothes . . .
   So early Tuesday morning.

4. This is the way we scrub the floor . . .
   So early Wednesday morning.

5. This is the way we mend our clothes . . .
   So early Thursday morning.

6. This is the way we sweep the house . . .
   So early Friday morning.

7. This is the way we bake our bread . . .
   So early Saturday morning.

8. This is the way we go to church . . .
   So early Sunday morning.

Nelly Bly

Starting note: Fifth string, second fret.

Stephen C. Foster

Nelly Bly has a voice like a turtle dove,
I hear it in the meadow and I hear it in the grove;
Nelly Bly has a heart warm as a cup of tea,
And bigger than the sweet potato down in Tennessee.
Chorus

Nelly Bly shuts her eye when she goes to sleep,
When she wakens up again her eyeballs 'gin to peep;
The way she walks, she lifts her foot, and then she brings it down,
And when it lights there's music there in that part of the town.
Chorus

Nelly Bly! Nelly Bly! Never, never sigh,
Never bring the tear drop to the corner of your eye;
For the pie is made of punkins and the mush is made of corn,
And there's corn and punkins plenty, love, lyin' in the barn.
Chorus

Oats, Peas, Beans, and Barley Grow

Starting note: Open second string.

Oats, peas, beans, and barley grow,
Oats, peas, beans, and barley grow;
Can you or I or anyone know
How oats, peas, beans, and barley grow?

Next the farmer waters the seed,
Then he stands and takes his ease;
He stamps his foot and claps his hands,
And turns around and views his lands.

Verse

The children form a ring, then circle around a child in the center who represents the farmer. During the second part of the chorus, the children imitate the farmer's motions in sowing, etc. Then they clasp hands again.

The dancing group again circles around the "farmer" while singing the first part of the verse. At the conclusion of the first part of the verse, the "farmer" chooses a partner, and they both kneel during the second part of the verse. Then the "farmer" joins the ring of children and the child he chose takes his place as the farmer.

Oh! Susanna

Starting note: Open third string.

Stephen Foster

Old Abe Lincoln Came out of the Wilderness

Starting note: Open fourth string.

Old Jeff Davis tore down the government,
Tore down the government, tore down the government;
Old Jeff Davis tore down the government,
Many long years ago.

Old Abe Lincoln built up a better one,
Built up a better one, built up a better one;
Old Abe Lincoln built up a better one,
Many long years ago.

Old Blue

Starting note: Second string, third fret.

There are many versions of this popular southern song. Although the chords are simple, the melody and its rhythm can vary considerably from one verse to the next; successful navigation of the tune relies on a certain amount of melodic improvisation.

Now old Blue bayed, and I went to see,
Blue had a 'possum up a 'simmon tree;
That possum come out on a swinging limb,
Blue barked at the possum and the 'possum growled at him.

Blue grinned at me,
And I winked at him;
I shook the 'possum down,
And Blue brought him in.
Chorus

Baked that 'possum good and brown,
Laid them sweet potatoes all around;
Saying, "Come on, Blue,
You can have some too."
Chorus

When old Blue died, he died so hard,
Shook the ground in my back yard;
I dug his grave with a silver spade,
Lowered him down with a golden chain.
Chorus

There's only one thing that bothers my mind,
Blue went to heaven, left me behind;
When I get to Heaven, first thing I'll do,
Grab my horn and blow for Blue.
Chorus

The Old Chisholm Trail

Starting note: Open fourth string.

Well come a - long, boys, and lis - ten to my tale, I'll

tell you 'bout my trou - bles on the Old Chis - holm Trail; Come a -

REFRAIN

ti - yi yip - py yip - py yea, yip - py yea, Come a -

ti - yi - yip - py yip - py yea!

I was born in Tucson in the year of '89,
I can ride any horse inside the Arizona line;
Refrain

With my ten-dollar horse and my twenty-dollar saddle,
I headed down to Texas for to punch longhorn cattle;
Refrain

It's beans for lunch and it's bacon for dinner,
I'll betcha they give better grub to the muleskinner;
Refrain

The cattle they moan and the sheepdog they do bark,
And the lonesome coyote's howlin on the praire in the dark;
Refrain

Old Dan Tucker

Starting note: Open third string.

Went to town the oth - er night to hear a noise and see a fight;

All the peo - ple were run - ning a - round, say - ing,

"Old Dan Tuck - er's a - com - in' to town.

Get out the way for Old Dan Tuck - er, He's too late to get his sup - per;

Sup - per's o - ver and din - ner's cook - in',

Old Dan Tuck - er's just stand - in' there look - in'.

Old Dan Tucker came to town
Riding a billy goat, leading a hound;
Hound, he barked and the billy goat jumped,
And throwed old Dan right straddle of a stump.
Chorus

Old Dan Tucker came to town,
Swingin' the ladies 'round and 'round;
First to the right and then to the left,
And then to the one you love the best.
Chorus

Old Dan Tucker's a fine old man,
Washed his face in a frying pan;
Combed his hair with a wagon wheel,
And died with a toothache in his heel.
Chorus

Old MacDonald Had a Farm

Starting note: Open third string.

Old Mac-Don-ald had a farm, E - I - E - I - O! And

on this farm he had a duck, E - I - E - I - O! With a
(some ducks,)

quack, quack here and a quack, quack there,

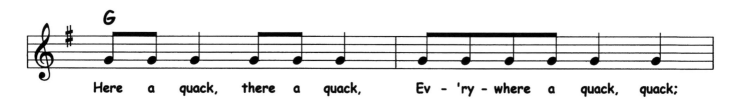

Here a quack, there a quack, Ev - 'ry - where a quack, quack;

Old Mac-Don-ald had a farm, E - I - E - I - O!

Chick . . . cluck, cluck

Cow . . . moo, moo

Pig . . . oink, oink

Cat . . . meow, meow

Horse . . . neigh, neigh

Dog . . . woof, woof

Etc.

Old Rattler

Starting note: Open third string.

Grand-pa had an old blind dog,__ Blind as he could be;

Ev - 'ry night at sup-per-time You'd think that dog could see.

Here, Rat - tler, here, here, Here, Rat__ - tler, here;

Call Rat - tler from the barn,__ Here, Rat__ - tler, here.

Took Rattler out the other night,
I thought he'd tree'd a coon;
I got there to find out
He was barkin' at the moon.
Chorus

Polly had a red-tail hen,
A-nestin' on the ground;
Set her on a dozen eggs
And out hatched a redbone hound.
Chorus

Grandpa had a muley cow,
Muley sure's you're born;
Took a jaybird forty years
To fly from horn to horn.
Chorus

Old Rattler's dead and gone,
Gone where good dogs go;
Better not be a dog yourself,
Or you'll be goin' there too.
Chorus

Old Smoky

Starting note: Open third string.

On top of old Smok - y,_____ All cov - ered with

snow;_____ I lost my true

lov - er_____ From a - court - in' too

slow._____

2. A-courtin's a pleasure,
   A-partin' is grief;
   A false-hearted lover
   Is worse than a thief.

3. A thief he will rob you,
   And take what you have;
   But a false-hearted lover
   Sends you to your grave.

4. They'll hug you and kiss you,
   And tell you more lies;
   Than the leaves on a willow,
   And stars in the skies.

5. The leaves they will wither,
   The roots they will die;
   You will be forsaken,
   And never know why.

6. Come all you fair maidens,
   Take warning from me;
   Don't place your affections
   On a green willow tree.

7. On top of Old Smoky,
   All covered with snow;
   I lost my true lover
   From a-courtin' too slow.

Over the River and Through the Woods

Starting note: Open fourth string.

Lydia Maria Child

O - ver the riv - er and through the woods to grand-moth-er's house we go,_____ The

horse knows the way to car - ry the sleigh, A - cross the drift - ing snow, O!

O - ver the riv - er and through the woods, Oh how the wind does blow,_____ It

stings the toes and bites the nose as o - ver the ground we go.

Over the river and through the woods,
To have a first-rate play;
Oh hear the bells ring, "Ting-a-ling-ling!"
Hurrah for Thanksgiving Day, Hey!
Over the river and through the woods,
Trot fast my dapple gray!
Spring over the ground, like a hunting hound!
For this is Thanksgiving Day, Hey!

Paper of Pins

Starting note: Open fourth string.

Boy 1. I'll give to you a pa - per of pins, For
Girl 2. I'll not ac - cept your pa - per of pins, If

that's the way that love be - gins; If
that's the way that love be - gins; And

you will mar - ry me, me, me, If
I'll not mar - ry you, you, you, And

you will mar_____ - ry me._____
I'll not mar_____ - ry you._____

Boy

3. I'll give to you a nice easy chair,
   To sit and comb your golden hair;
   If you will marry me, me, me,
   If you will marry me.

5. I'll give to you a fine dress of green,
   To make you look just like a real queen;
   If you will marry me, me, me,
   If you will marry me.

7. I'll give to you the key to my heart,
   That we may love and never part;
   If you will marry me, me, me,
   If you will marry me.

Girl

4. I'll not accept your nice easy chair,
   To sit and comb my golden hair;
   And I'll not marry you, you, you,
   And I'll not marry you.

6. I'll not accept your fine dress of green,
   To make me look just like a real queen;
   And I'll not marry you, you, you,
   And I'll not marry you.

8. Yes, I'll accept the key to your heart,
   That we may love and never part;
   And I will marry you, you, you,
   And I will marry you.

Pick a Bale of Cotton

Starting note: Open second string.

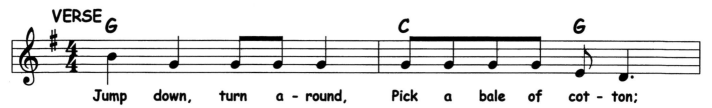

Jump down, turn a - round, Pick a bale of cot - ton;

Jump down, turn a - round, Pick a bale a day.

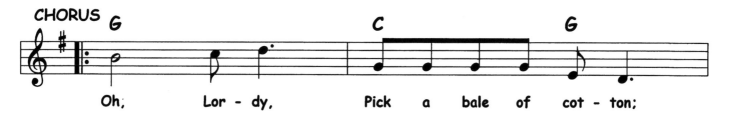

Oh; Lor - dy, Pick a bale of cot - ton;

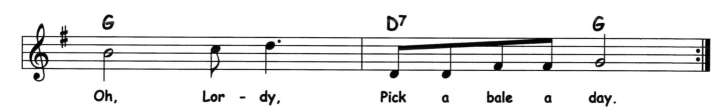

Oh, Lor - dy, Pick a bale a day.

Takes a mighty man
To pick a bale of cotton;
Takes a mighty man
To pick a bale a day. (2x)
Chorus (2x)

Me and my buddy
Gonna pick a bale of cotton;
Me and my buddy
Gonna pick a bale a day. (2x)
Chorus (2x)

Me and my good gal
Can pick a bale of cotton . . .

Little Julie Johnson
Can pick a bale of cotton . . .

Etc.

The Pine Tree

Starting note: Open fourth string.

O mountain pine, O mountain pine,
On high thou watchest o'er us,
mountain pine, O mountain pine,
How faithful art thou ever;
Thou art as green in winter's snow,
As in the summer's richest glow,
O mountain pine, O mountain pine,
How faithful art thou ever.

Polly, Put the Kettle On

Starting note: Second string, third fret.

Pol - ly, put the ket - tle on, Pol - ly put the ket - tle on;

Pol - ly, put the ket - tle on, We'll all have tea.

Su - key, take it off a - gain, Su - key, take it off a - gain;

Su - key, take it off a - gain, They're all gone a - way.

Polly Wolly Doodle

Starting note: Open third string.

Oh, my Sal she am a maiden fair,
Singing Polly Wolly Doodle all the day;
With curly eyes and laughing hair,
Sing Polly Wolly Doodle all the day.
Chorus

Pretty Little Girl with a Red Dress On

Starting note: Fifth string, second fret.

As in all folk songs, many lyrical variations are possible: blue dress, straw hat, green skirt, etc.

Railroad Bill

Starting note: Second string, third fret.

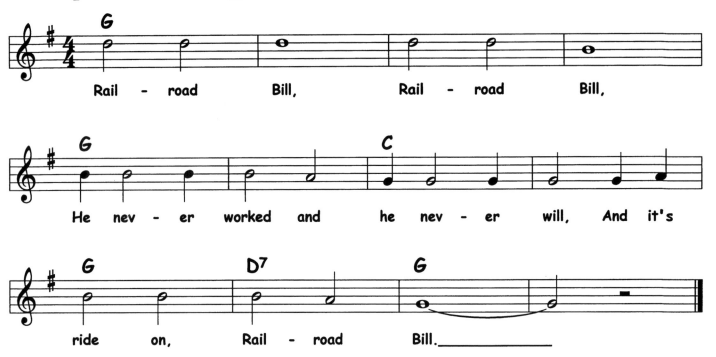

Rail - road Bill, Rail - road Bill,

He nev - er worked and he nev - er will, And it's

ride on, Rail - road Bill._____

Railroad Bill goin' over the hill,
Lightin' cigars with a ten-dollar bill,
And it's ride on, Railroad Bill.

Railroad Bill was a mighty big sport,
Shot all the buttons off the sheriff's coat,
And it's ride on, Railroad Bill.

Kill me a chicken, send me the wing,
Folks think I'm working', but I ain't doin' a thing,
And it's ride on, Railroad Bill.

Reuben and Rachel

Starting note: Open third string.

Rachel: Reu - ben,   I   have   long been think - ing   What   a   good world   this would be;
Reuben: Rach - el,   I   have   long been think - ing   What   a   fine world   this might be;

If   the   men   were   all trans - port - ed   far be__ - yond   the   North - ern Sea.
If   we   had   some   more young la - dies   On this__   side   the   North - ern Sea.

Reuben, Reuben, I've been thinking
What a great life girls would lead;
If they had no men about them,
None to tease them, none to heed.

Rachel, Rachel, I've been thinking
Life would be so easy then;
What a lovely world this would be
If you'd leave it to the men.

Reuben, Reuben, stop your teasing
If you've any love for me;
I was only just a-fooling
As I thought, of course, you'd see.

Rachel, if you'll not transport us
I will take you for my wife;
And I'll split with you my money
Every pay day of my life!

The Riddle Song

Starting note: Open fourth string.

How can there be a cherry that has no stone?
How can there be a chicken that has no bone?
How can there be a story that has no end?
How can there be a baby with no cryin'?

A cherry when in blossom, it has no stone,
A chicken in the egg it has no bone;
The story that I love you, it has no end,
And when a baby's sleepin', there's no cryin'.

Ring Around a Rosy

Starting note: Open third string.

All the players dance around in a ring, and fall down at the last words.

Robinson Crusoe

Starting note: Open second string.

1. When I was a lad, I had cause to be sad, A
2. He saved from a-board an old gun and a sword, And a-

ver-y good friend I did lose, O! I
noth-er odd mat-ter or two; So by

war-rant you, Dan, you have heard of this man, His
dint of his thrift, he just man-aged to shift, And

name it was Rob-in-son Cru-soe.
keep a-live Rob-in-son Cru-soe.

CHORUS

Oh, Rob-in-son Cru-soe!
Oh, Rob-in-son Cru-soe!

Oh, poor Rob-in-son Cru-soe! He_____
Oh, poor Rob-in-son Cru-soe! Wheth-er

went off to sea and be-tween you and me, Old
tem-pest or Turk,_____ or wild man or work,

Nep-tune wreck'd Rob-in-son Cru-soe.
mat-ter to Rob-in-son Cru-soe.

Rock-A-Bye Baby

Starting note: Fifth string, second fret.

Mother Goose's Melodies (1765)
Effie I. Canning (1884)

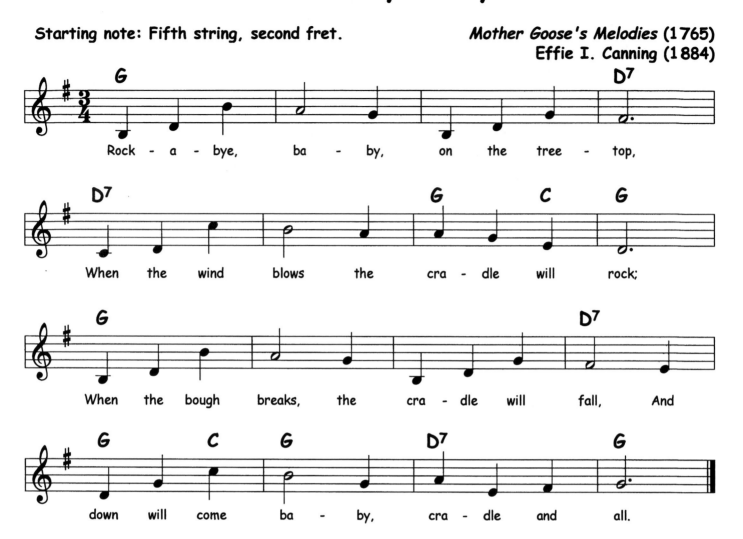

Rock - a - bye, ba - by, on the tree - top,

When the wind blows the cra - dle will rock;

When the bough breaks, the cra - dle will fall, And

down will come ba - by, cra - dle and all.

Rock-A-Bye Baby

Starting note: Open second string.

Mother Goose's Melodies, (1765)
Alfred S. Gatty

1. Rock - a - bye, ba - by on the tree top,
2. Hush - a - bye, ba - by up in the sky,

When the wind blows the cra - dle will rock;
On a soft cloud 'tis ea - sy to fly;

When the bough breaks the cra - dle will fall,
When the cloud bursts the rain - drops will pour,

Down will come ba - by, cra - dle and all.
Ba - by comes down to mo - ther once more.

Rock That Cradle, Lucy

Starting note: Open third string.

Rock   that   Cra - dle   Lu - cy,

Rock   that   cra - dle   long;

Rock   that   cra - dle   Lu - cy,

Keep   that   ba - by   warm.

Rock that cradle Lucy, rock that cradle spry;
Rock that cradle Lucy, don't let that baby cry.

Rock that cradle Lucy, rock it Lucy long;
Rock that cradle Lucy, keep that baby warm.

Rock that cradle Lucy, rock that cradle spry;
Rock that cradle Lucy, don't let that baby cry.

Round and Round the Village

Starting note: Open second string.

Round and round the vil - lage,
Round and round the vil - lage;
Round and round the vil - lage, As
we have done be - fore.

In and out the windows,	Kiss her 'fore you leave her,	Stand and face your partner,
In and out the windows;	Kiss her 'fore you leave her;	Stand and face your partner;
In and out the windows,	Kiss her 'fore you leave her,	Stand and face your partner,
As we have done before.	As we have done before.	As we have done before.

The children form a ring with one player on the outside, who runs around it while they are singing. During the second verse they raise their arms to let her in the center, and she runs in and out between the children, trying to complete the circle before the verse ends.

In the third verse, she chooses her partner and they stand facing each other until the fourth verse when they exchange a kiss. Then the game begins all over again with the first child back in the circle and the one who was chosen as the partner on the outside.

Sally Goodin

Starting note: Open third string.

Had a piece of pie, And I had a piece of pud - din', And I

gave it all a - way, Just to see my Sal - ly Good - in'.

I look'd down the road, And I see my Sal - ly com - in', And I

thought__ to my soul__ that I'd kill my - self a - run - nin'.

Love a 'tater pie and I love an apple puddin',
And I love a little gal that they call Sally Goodin.
Love a 'tater pie and I love an apple puddin',
And I love a little gal that they call Sally Goodin.
Dropped The 'tater pie and I left the apple puddin',
But I went across the mountain just to see my Sally Goodin.
Dropped The 'tater pie and I left the apple puddin',
But I went across the mountain just to see my Sally Goodin.

Sally Go 'Round the Sun

Starting note: Open third string.

Sal - ly go 'round the sun,

Sal - ly go 'round the moon;

Sal - ly go 'round the sun - shine

Ev - 'ry aft - er - noon. Boom! Boom!

Sandy Land

Starting note: Open second string.

Sift that flour____ and save the bran,

Ba - con fry - in' up in the pan;

Bake them bis - cuits and spread the jam,

Eve - ry - bod - y's hap - py in Sand - y Land.

Play that fiddle and clap your hands,
Chickens lay eggs and scratch the land;
Fetch up a hog and save the ham,
Everybody's happy in Sandy Land.

Got me a coonhound, black and tan,
Best rabbit dog in all the land;
Trees him up a coon everytime he can,
Everybody's happy in Sandy Land.

Shoo Fly

Starting note: Open second string.

Shoo fly, don't both-er me, Shoo fly, don't both-er me;

Shoo fly, don't both-er me, For I be-long to some-bod-y. I

feel, I feel, I feel like a morn-ing star; I

feel, I feel, I feel like a morn-ing star.

Shoo fly, don't both-er me, Shoo fly, don't both-er me;

Shoo fly, don't both-er me, For I be-long to some-body-y.

Short'nin' Bread

Starting note: Open third string.

Three little children lyin' in bed
Two was sick and the other 'most dead;
Sent for the doctor, and the doctor said,
"Give them children some short'nin' bread."
Chorus

I slipped in the kitchen, an' slipped up the led,*
I slipped up my pockets full of short'nin' bread;
I stole the skillet, I stole the led,
And I stole the gal who makes short'nin' bread.
Chorus

They caught me with the skillet, they caught me with the led,
They caught me with the gal cookin' short'nin' bread;
Paid for de skillet, paid for the led,
Went straight to jail for eatin' short'nin' bread.
Chorus

* Lid

Sing a Song of Sixpence

Starting note: Second string, third fret.

1. __ Sing a song of six - pence, A pock - et full of rye,
2. The King was in the count-ing house, Count -ing out his mon-ey, The

four - and twen - ty black - birds Bak'd in a pie;
Queen was in the par - lor, Eat - ing bread and hon - ey; The

When the pie was o - pen'd, The birds be - gan to sing,
maid was in the gar - den Hang - ing out the clothes,

Was - n't that a dain - ty dish to set be - fore a King?
Down____ came a black____ - bird and peck'd___ off her nose.

Sing Song Kitty

Starting note: Open third string.

Additional lyrics (verses may be sung in any order)

Way down yonder and not far off,
Sing song kitty kitchie ki-me-o;
A jaybird died with the whoppin' cough,
Sing song kitty kitchie ki-me-o.
Chorus

My cow won't give the milk in the summer,
Sing song kitty kitchie ki-me-o;
So we've got to take it from her,
Sing song kitty kitchie ki-me-o.
Chorus

Mama's in the garden siftin' sand,
Sing song kitty kitchie ki-me-o;
Sal's in love with a hog-eyed man,
Sing song kitty kitchie ki-me-o.
Chorus

Sleep, Baby, Sleep!

Starting note: Open second string.

Sleep, baby, sleep!	Sleep, baby, sleep!	Sleep, baby, sleep!
I would not, would not weep;	Near where the woodbines creep;	Thy rest shall angels keep;
The little lamb he never cries,	Be always like the lamb so mild,	While on the grass the lamb shall feed,
And bright and happy are his eyes;	A sweet, and kind, and gentle child;	And never suffer want or need;
Sleep, baby, sleep!	Sleep, baby, sleep!	Sleep, baby, sleep!

Sleep, Sleep, My Darling
(French Lullaby)

Starting note: Open second string.

1. Sleep, sleep, my dar____ - ling, sleep peace - ful - ly,
2. Sleep, sleep, my dar____ - ling, sleep peace - ful - ly,

Moth - er is watch____ - ing, pray - ing for thee;
Thy lov - ing fa____ - ther car - eth for thee,

May ho - ly an - gels on wings of light,
In thy soft cra - dle, peace - ful - ly sleep,

Bring to my ba____ - by, dreams fair and bright.
While thou dost slum____ - ber, watch he will keep.

Do - do, my dar - ling, peace - ful - ly sleep.
Do - do, my dar - ling, peace - ful - ly sleep.

Slumber Song

Starting note: Open second string.

Soldier, Soldier, Will You Marry Me?

Starting note: Open third string.

Sol - dier, sol - dier, will you mar - ry me, With your knap - sack, fife and drum? "Oh

how can I mar - ry such a pret - ty maid as thee, When I've got no coat to put on?" Then she

REFRAIN

ran a - way to the tai___-lor's___ shop, As fast as she could run; And she

bought him a coat of the ve - ry, ve - ry best, and the sol - dier put it on.

2. Soldier, soldier, will you marry me,
   With your knapsack, fife and drum?
   "Oh, how can I marry such a pretty maid as thee,
   When I have no shoes to put on?"
   Then she ran away to the shoemaker's shop,
   As fast as she could run;
   And she bought him a pair of the very, very best,
   And the soldier put them on.

3. Soldier, soldier, will you marry me,
   With your knapsack, fife and drum?
   "Oh, how can I marry such a pretty maid as thee,
   When I have no hat to put on?"
   Then she ran away to the hat maker's shop,
   As fast as she could run;
   And she bought him a pair of the very, very best,
   And the soldier put them on.

4. Soldier, soldier, will you marry me,
   With your knapsack, fife and drum?
   "Oh, how can I marry such a pretty maid as thee,
   When I have no gloves to put on?"
   Then she ran away to the glove-maker's shop,
   As fast as she could run;
   And she bought him a pair of the very, very best,
   And the soldier put them on.

5. Soldier, soldier, will you marry me,
   With your knapsack, fife and drum?
   "Oh, how can I marry such a pretty maid as thee,
   When I've got a good wife at home?"

Two children are selected to play the parts.
The little girl sings the first half of the verse
and the little boy the second. When he says he
has no coat to put on, she borrows one from
one of the other children, and so on for each verse.
No refrain after the soldier's part of verse 5.

The Sow Took the Measles

Starting note: Open second string.

CHORUS
How do you think I be - gan in the world? Well, I got me a sow and sev - 'ral oth - er things. The sow took the mea-sles, and died in the spring.

VERSE
What do you think I made of her hide? The ver - y best sad - dle that you ev - er did ride. Sad - dle or bri - dle or an - y such thing, The sow took the mea-sles, and died in the spring.

What do you think I made of her nose?
The very best thimble that ever sewed clothes.
Thimble or thread or any such thing,
The sow took the measles, and died in the spring.

What do you think I made of her tail?
The very best whup that ever sought sail.
Whup or whup socket, or any such thing,
The sow took the measles, and died in the spring.

What do you think I made of her feet?
The very best pickles that you ever did eat.
Pickles or glue or any such thing,
The sow took the measles, and died in the spring.

This early American song starts with the chorus, after which the verses may be interchanged in any manner. In some arrangements, the chorus is sung only at the very beginning.

Suzanna Gal

Starting note: Open second string.

Cof - fee grows on white oak trees, Riv - er flows with bran - dy;

If I had my pret - ty li'l miss I'd feed her sug - ar can - dy.

Fly a - round my pret - ty li'l miss, Fly a - round my dai - sy;

Fly a - round my pret - ty li'l miss, You al - most drive me cra - zy.

Cheeks as red as a blooming rose,
Eyes of the prettiest brown;
I'm goin' to see my pretty little miss
Before the sun goes down.
Chorus

Where are you goin my pretty little miss,
Where are you goin my daisy?
Oh, if I don't get me a young man soon
I think I'm a-goin crazy.
Chorus

Cheeks as red as a blooming rose,
Eyes of the prettiest brown;
I'm goin' to see my pretty little miss
Before the sun goes down.
Chorus

Ten Little Kangaroos

Starting note: Open third string.

One lit - tle, two lit - tle, three lit - tle kan - ga - roos,

Four lit - tle, five lit - tle, six lit - tle kan - ga - roos;

Sev'n lit - tle, eight lit - tle, nine lit - tle kan - ga - roos,

Ten lit - tle kan - ga - roos.

Ten little, nine little, eight little kangaroos,
Sev'n little, six little, five little kangaroos;
Four little, three little, two little kangaroos,
One little kangaroo.

While singing the first verse, the children appear suddenly one by one, hopping kangaroo fashion. In the second verse, they disappear one by one the same way.

There's Music in the Air

Starting note: Open fourth string.

George F. Root

1. There's mu - sic in the air_____ When the in-fant morn is nigh, And
2. There's mu - sic in the air_____ When the moon-tide's sul-try beam Re -

faint its blush is seen_____ On the bright and laugh - ing sky.
flects a gold - en light_____ On the dis-tant moun - tain stream.

Man - y a harp's ec - stat - ic sound, With its thrill of joy pro - found,
When be - neath some grate - ful shade, Sor - row's ach - ing head is laid,

While we list en - chant - ed there, To the mu - sic in the air.
Sweet - ly to the spir - it there, Comes the mu - sic in the air.

Three Little Kittens

Starting note: Open fourth string.

1. Once three lit-tle kit-tens they lost their mit-tens, And they be-gan to cry,_____ Oh!
2. The three lit-tle kit-tens they found their mit-tens, And they be-gan to cry,_____ Oh!
3. The three lit-tle kit-tens put on their mit-tens, And soon ate up the pie;_____ Oh!,

mam - my dear, we sad - ly fear, Our mit - tens we have lost;_____ What,
mam - my dear, see here, see here, Our mit - tens we have foun;_____ What,
Mam - my dear, see here, see here, Our mit - tens we have soil'd._____ What,

lost your mit-tens, you naugh - ty kit - tens, Then you shall have no pie._____
found your mit-tens, you dar - ling kit - tens, Then you shall have some pie._____
soil'd your mit-tens, you naugh - ty kit - tens, Then they be - gan to sigh._____

REFRAIN

Mi - ew, mi - ew, mi - ew, mi - ew;

Mi - ew, mi - ew, mi - ew, miew._____

Three Sight-Challenged Mice

Starting note: Open second string.

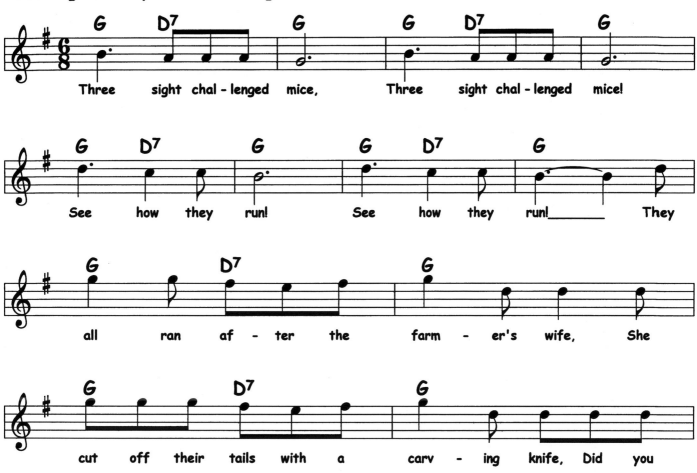

Three sight chal - lenged mice, Three sight chal - lenged mice!

See how they run! See how they run!_____ They

all ran af - ter the farm - er's wife, She

cut off their tails with a carv - ing knife, Did you

ev - er see such a sight in your life as

three sight chal - lenged mice?

Tirra-Lirra-Lirra

Starting note: Second string, third fret.

Tirra-lirra-lirra is our song,
When the lovely summer days are long;
Rowing on the river or the sea,
Tirra-lirra-lirra, sing with glee.

Tirra-lirra-lirra, soft and low,
Hear the brook in winter 'neath the snow;
Tho' the leaves are dead wher'e'r we look,
"Tirra-lirra-lirra," sings the brook.

Welcome to Spring

Starting note: Open third string.

What Can the Matter Be?

Starting note: Second string, third fret.

When I Was a Lady

Starting note: Second string, third fret.

When I was a young girl . . .

When I was a young man . . .

When I was a dancer . . .

When I was a soldier . . .

A leader is chosen for the first verse, and she initiates the actions of a
lady by making a curtsey and kissing her hands, first right and then left.
A different child is chosen to represent the character in each of the verses
and the other children imitate whatever motions they make.

Winter Waltz

L.M.

Starting note: Open second string.

Snow - capped pines and frost - y bree - zes,

Ma - ry shiv - ers, Jim - my snee - zes;

Moth - er pleads, "Please but - ton up," It's

time for a win - ter waltz._____

Old men grow their beards down low,
To help block out the flakes of snow;
Swede lumberjacks wear checkered coats,
It's time for a winter waltz.

Little sis dons fuzzy mittens,
Brother aims packed ice at kittens;
Father shrugs and scrapes the van,
It's time for a winter waltz.

Gingerbread has lovely fragrance,
Old Maid teacher tumbles down;
Blind snowman stares from charcoal eyes,
It's time for a winter waltz.

It's time for a winter waltz.

Ye Maids of Helston
(Cornish May Song)

Starting note: Open fourth string.